And We Were Sailors...

And We Were Sailors...

Poetry & Essays

David L. Benson

killick press
an imprint of Creative Publishers

St. John's, Newfoundland
2002

Le Conseil des Arts | The Canada Council
du Canada | for the Arts

We acknowledge the support of The Canada Council for the Arts for our publishing
program.

We acknowledge the financial support of the Government of Canada through the Book
Publishing Industry Development Program (BPIDP) for our publishing
program.

Front Cover Art: David L. Benson (photo of sea ice off northern Newfoundland)
Back Cover Art: Tapestry by Catherine McCausland (Photo taken by Ned Pratt)

∞ Printed on acid-free paper

Published by
KILLICK PRESS
an imprint of CREATIVE BOOK PUBLISHING
a division of 10366 Newfoundland Limited
a Robinson-Blackmore Printing & Publishing associated company
P.O. Box 8660, St. John's, Newfoundland A1B 3T7

First Edition
Typeset in 11.5 point Galliard BT

Printed in Canada by:
ROBINSON-BLACKMORE PRINTING & PUBLISHING

National Library of Canada Cataloguing in Publication Data

Benson, David L., 1956–
    And we were sailors... : poetry & essays

ISBN 1-894294-41-6

    1. Newfoundland-Poetry. 2. Protest poetry, Canadian (English)—
Newfoundland. I. Title.

PS8553.E558A8 2002   C811'.6   C2002-900682-1
PR9199.4.B46A8 2002

To Julie and all the Sarahs

Acknowledgments

Dawn Roche, Dwayne LaFitte and Gordon Rodgers, without whose kindness, patience, professionalism and understanding, this book would never have been published. My parents, Lindsay, and the late Sarah (Pardy) Benson, without whom it would never have been conceived, my only brother Ron, the Rev. Koten Benson, without whom it would never have been printable, Julie (Skinner) Woodman of Boxey and Lily (Carter) Benson of Greenspond, without whom it would never have been written, and my artistic daughter Sarah Ann, eleven years old and writing her own poems, my technically minded son, Thomas Lindsay, who, at the age of four, knows the difference between a sloop and a schooner, and my indomitable wife, Catherine McCausland, for whom fulsome praise would be so much meaningless flattery when compared to the love, honour and respect in which I hold her, and without whom it would never have been possible.

Contents

FENCES ON THE LANDWASH

WINTER OF THE RALS

AFTERWORD

Foreword

Beach Woman
(For my Great Great Grandmother)

I never knew her,
but through a photograph
taken when she was ninety three:
hard lined eyes and fearless face,
on her way to the beach to gather kelp.
Big hands in mitts and a brin bag
folded over her arm.

Emma Blagdon.
She belonged to Jack's Fountain
and came to live in Boxey.

Pulled turnips, kept sheep,
delivered babies like her Mother
and her Mother's Mother,

back through the fog of unwritten history
to places uncharted
and names they left in coves of hazy memories.
Made fish, made splits,
trimmed the lamps and all between,
when the men were away, dying in dories.

Kept up her half of the fishery.

The Colour Of My Flag

I was born in St. John's on July 19, 1956, when my family lived on the Southside. I grew up there and on Torbay Road, then on the city's periphery, finished high school and after one term at Memorial University, when to sea at age 17.

My Father was a longshoreman, the son of a longshoreman from the Southside. His Grandfather came to St. John's from Grates Cove where the Bensons had lived since the early 1800s, coming originally from Carbonear, and it is emblematic that the only word he pronounces with a Conception Bay North accent is "work". His Grandmother, from Bay de Verde, was a traditional healer and known as a witch. A great uncle died at Cambrai in World War I. Another great uncle was one of the legendary "Fish" who helped build the skyscrapers of New York in the 1920s.

My Grandmother was the. daughter of a sealer-shipwright. Her people, including the Greens of Pond, were the earliest planters of Bonavista North. The first of her ancestors connected with Newfoundland was John Carter in 1498 and another, William Carter, was a leader in the livyere's fight against the West County English fishermen in the late 1600s. My ancestors include the sealing Captains Thomas, Darius and Daniel Green, W.S. Bemister, Charles and Peter Carter. In 1933, Peter, commanding the S.S. *Ungava*, landed the heaviest load of seals in history.

My Mother was a teacher, a Pardy from Grand Bank whose family had been in Fortune Bay since the early 1800s. They were in Burin in the 1700s and in Placentia in the 1600s. (Pardy's Island in Burin and Paradise — originally Pardy's Harbour, attest to their early connections.) Her close relatives include Captains Joe Barnes, Robert and John Smith (the 77 year old sailor in the replica *Matthew*) and Captain Alec Smith, "The Fish Killer" of Harbour Mille. Her Father was in the schooner *Robert Max* when she was sunk by *U125* in 1941.

Her Grandfather was lost in the schooner *Tubal Cain* in

1907. Her Mother, from Boxey, worked in service in Grand Bank and died of tuberculosis at the age of 38 and her Grandfather, Tommy Baker, from Lally Cove, drowned while fishing crosshanded off Stone's Head. Her Grandmother's first husband was Isaac Skinner of Boxey. Their son, Isaac Jr., nicknamed "Ike Jones", was Master of the schooner *Marion*, made famous by "Simani", two of my Mother's cousins.

My Aunt, Julie Skinner, was one of the women who saved American sailors from the wrecks of *Pollux* and *Truxton*. My Great Great Grandmother, Emma Blagdon, was a midwife and senior hand of the Beach Women of Boxey, still working in her 90s.

My sixth generation Great Grandfather, James Miles, was the first livyere at Head of Fortune Bay in the late 1700s and was interviewed by Archdeacon Wix during his famous travels in the area in 1832. The Maid of Honour at my parent's wedding was Maude Pittman, daughter of "The Fighting Newfoundlander", Corporal Thomas Pittman.

I am a Newfoundlander, descended from the "copper-coloured" Bush Borns, the early livyeres. I don't consider myself a British or Irish colonial, nor perhaps even a Canadian. I am, however, an internationalist and find much in common with Norwegian, Russian, Spanish, French or Icelandic fishermen, despite the obvious linguistic and apparent cultural differences.

Politically, I was moulded by the best mentors to be had; the arrogant and ignorant ruling class of Newfoundland and their treacherous political puppets. I was five years old when my family was forced off the Southside and as a result, came to have little use for those in power who thought they deserved my respect merely for their titles. Though I was never a "problem student", my first "act of rebellion", usually associated with one's teenage years, occurred on my first day in Kindergarten.

My primary interests in school were History and Geography, but I have always been interested in words, the sound of language, the idea of speech and the hard comfort of books. Today, I have three bookshelves worth of dictionaries.

Two teachers stand out; both in High School. Bertram Brown in Literature and Beniah Hicks in History were invaluable. Mr. Brown, whose eloquence was such that he might have conducted classes in top hat and cape, encouraged my love of language and Mr. Hicks encouraged critical thought, particularly in matters as presented by the media and those in authority. To both of these gentlemen, and they really were gentlemen, I owe a great deal.

My Mother read to me and encouraged me to read at an early age. She often took my brother and me to the library and by the time I was nine, was taking books out of the adult library.

Perhaps it was from reading non-fiction early in life that I acquired my writing style, succinct and without much embellishment, although written in a form that is somewhat anachronistic and tends to make me appear older than I am. But then, I started writing early too. My first Letter to the Editor, the first of possibly hundreds, was written when I was 13.

Turning to poetry was probably the rationalization for ineptitude with punctuation. And I now recognize that what I began with, was really stacked prose. However, learning the work of Twentieth century American poets in school (of course, we never learned of the great Newfoundland poets; Irving Fogwill, Isaac Newell, the Horwoods, Greg Power and the rest) there seemed no rhyme nor rhythm to modern poetry. Fogwill's "Appeal to Parnassus", Harold Horwood's "To The Owners Of The Wheels" and Newell's "Lines For An Anniversary" would have inspired me to think that, as a Newfoundlander, I might be able to write. Alas, there was none of that. A Newfoundlander poet was simply unthinkable. When, following High School, I read Enos Watts, Paul O'Neill, Tom Dawe and others, I thought that they represented the beginning of Newfoundland poetry. I know now that this was not the case.

After Grade XI, I had a furtive look into university and went to sea with the navy out of Halifax and Esquimalt. There, I educated myself, read all that was available and affordable and discovered the existence of the second hand bookstore. I travelled across the North Atlantic several times, sailed the Pacific, the Mediterranean, Caribbean, North and Barents Seas, visited over a dozen countries and saw life there, not from a window of a tour bus or a hotel balcony, but in seaport bars, backstreets and brothels, saw the inside of a cruise liner, not as a passenger but as an impromptu guest of the crew, went horseback riding in Jamaica, drank beer inside a dumpster in Pearl Harbour and visited a Buddhist temple, wandered around the Catacombs in Rome and saw the Sistine Chapel, took the wrong bus and ended up in Pompeii, witnessed the Portuguese Revolution and Franco's Spain, came near to losing my careless life on at least three occasions (that I can remember) and generally had a good time of it. All the while, I read: History, Politics, Religion, Sociology, Mythology, novels, essays and poetry. Sailors read. It is a natural law of the universe.

I stopped going to sea in 1978 and went to work on-shore for a large fishing company. There I met some of the great fishermen and vessel Captains of Newfoundland. After that, I was a newspaper reporter, and for a time, a contract and freelance writer and journalist.

I accidentally became a bartender in a late-night downtown St. John's bar and was, for a time, a night watchman, "on the docks". During these years, I had occasion to meet and experience some of the most interesting people outside of Science Fiction.

For the past 14 years, I have worked as an International Fisheries Observer in Russian, Estonian, French, Norwegian, Icelandic and Newfoundland vessels.

At sea after a ten year absence, I saw the sky again, became aware again of sunsets, became a mind delivered by stars. And I remembered why a 'literary Don' once told Captain Allan Villiers, "The few sailors who do write, can write." At sea, one sees sights incredible, reads everything imaginable and dreams vividly.

A ship is a microcosm of its country's society. Working aboard a foreign fishing vessel is "immersion" taken to its ultimate conclusion. But seamen are essentially the same everywhere; stoic fatalists with a high sense of honour and a twisted sense of humour. It is said we are a superstitious lot, but we live and work in an environment that often defies superlatives. And we quickly come to understand, as human beings, just how insignificant we are in the universe.

During trips to sea, which can last up to three months, I read, sometimes deliberately, as when I took the collected works of Byron, Shelley, Coleridge and Blake to the Flemish Cap, and more often haphazardly from an eclectic mixture of books. These cover subjects determined by interest or ignorance. An Atlas and a good dictionary are essential for any trip.

As with any writer, I am influenced by those I read, both in style and content. Sam Clemens, the 19th century American social critic, is too colloquial for my taste, yet there is a timeless attraction to the rapier acerbity of his "pen warmed up in Hell". And I'll always remember his admonition, "use the right word; not its second cousin." And George Orwell's straightforward political honesty is refreshing. Over the past ten years, I have discovered the vitriolic writings of Robert John Parsons; newspaper editor, political commentator, orator and 19th century Newfoundland statesman.

Among the poets, I most respect those who say something through their poetry, who, in the words of Irving Fogwill, "come down from the heights to the dirty towns ... To the laughter and tears where sins are sown".

Perhaps that is why I gravitated to the Russians. Yevgeny Yevtushenko said that "to write only of nature or Weltschmerz at a time of hardship for your people is almost amoral."

Poetry is too vital, too rarely published, to waste everyone's time with sonorous platitudes, esoteric musings or mawkish fluff and bluff. And to quote from yet another Russian; Vladimir Mayakovksy, a line which I try to keep as my maxim; "I want the pen to be equated with the bayonet."

I send poems to both literary journals and popular periodicals, including community newspapers and whatever new or alternative local magazines come along. Some 20 years ago, I sold single sheets of my poetry and songs on the street, at flea markets and at the Regatta to raise money for a political magazine. I've also posted up poems as posters, commenting on political matters and performed my work at Folk Festivals, various Benefits and other venues such as the Eastern Edge Gallery and the first Peace-A-Chord.

The Newfoundland Writer's Guild provided me with the first opportunity to read in public and since then, the Writer's Alliance Open Readings have been a great forum to try out new works and to try to improve my public speaking skills.

Letters to the Editor, essays, reviews, guest columns (Daily News, Vancouver Province and Ottawa Citizen) are a continuation of poetry "by other means", but poetry is also a continuation of politics. And no one who has read me is in any doubt as to the colour of my flag. During the life of the weekly Southern Post, I wrote a regular political column entitled "The Long Run".

My time ashore is somewhat limited and, by necessity, family responsibilities take up much of it. Between trips, I try to clean up poems and expand on notes written at sea.

I am married to the St. John's artisan and writer Catherine McCausland and we have two children. Over a nine year relationship, which began with words and in which words form an integral part, Catherine has become my Editor and civilizing conscience. We constantly discuss events and ideas. Unafraid to express herself politically in her own work, she has been fearless in her criticism of mine, though less critical, overall, than I am myself. In this, as in everything, her partnership has been both wondrous and crucial.

I am Secretary of the Local Service District of Tors Cove and a Shop Steward for the Fisheries Observer's union, International Brotherhood of Teamsters, Local 855.

For relaxation, I read in bed with my wife, or go in the woods.

I

. . . cold as the sea . . .

Navigator

Give me the Sun and Polaris,
a decent watch set to Greenwich —
I'll know where I am on the planet.

North of the Line, at least.
West of the Prime, anyway.
In Newfoundland, at least,
where the sea is brooding and grey
and the hills
are purple in May.

Is My Love Cold?
(For my Great Great Grandfather)

Is my love cold tonight,
alone in her bed,
woken by the wind tonight,
or dreams in her head?

Is my love cold tonight,
rocking in her chair,
waiting for the sound tonight,
sodden boots on her stair?

Is my child cold tonight,
crying in her room,
seeing through her tears tonight,
my wet face in the gloom?

For I am cold as the sea tonight,
the sea, west of Cape Finisterre.
And home I have returned tonight —
the fetch of Darius Bemister.

Isolation

We build this island
around the wash of the Great Bays,
scorning overland travel,
preferring perhaps the security of boats.
The bays became nations,
the rockbound places — City States.

Isolated?

Our Grandfathers travelled more than we do.
Persian rugs and Greek urns
adorned front rooms of houses
where women scanned the sea
with German telescopes for their return;
rough men and hard,
with delicate print dresses folded
over forearms thick from work in salted cold
and porcelain headed dolls
tucked beneath tarpaulin coats.

Yet there are those today who wax
warmly about "our culture",
who have been as far as Toronto,
who are scared to death of boats,
who call those people isolated.

They rowed across Fortune Bay in five hours or so.
Now we go by car and it takes us ten.

What do we know of the back street
politics of Naples or Lisbon,
or the price of tea in China?

Out Again

Green to blue and then to grey,
sea and sky become one
and there is no horizon save the stars.

Eternal ocean rolls
on past our pitching bows
and seabirds wheel and glide,
unending quest
as we too search
for food from out these depths.

We hunt the barrens and gullies
of this water planet,
to feed our families, clung
to rocky outcrops
above the deep.

Evening

Around us wallows the fleet;
our sisters, our partners
in this mad enterprise.

Darkling shapes,
now lifting close,
now falling away.

Each a little village,
safe behind her waltzing lights.

Iced Up

She is sluggish and rolls
tender now, like a careful drunk.
The foredeck is a white field.
The wheelhouse glistens,
a giant wedding cake adrift
in a turgid sea.
Spray has frozen
streaming from the windows.
Guardrails are a solid barricade,
perceptibly growing —
half inch wire;
big around as a barrel.

"Makin' ice, I believe, Skipper, b'y."
"That's right, old dear.
'Ave to get this off 'er later on,
I s'pose."

Blue Mist rolls heavily through my mind
and is gone.
He lost people on her. So did I.

"Goin' below for tea, Skipper."
"Finest kind, old dear.
Fill up me mug, would you?"

Tail of the Bank

Water slaps the wooden hull.
In the galley, round the table
where we eat, sleep, live,
sweat and freeze,
jammed against the bunkboards,
against the roll — drinking tea,
eating crackers.
Pay the knife with butter,
slap it down on a cracker,
twist the knife, slap another cracker —
up to the mouth and gone.
Gannetized!
As my Grandfather did.
The wind comes around
and we run off before it —
cupboard door breaks its latch
and swings on noisome hinges,
strikes again, again.
In the morning, gillnets
wind creaking aboard,
twisting under the gurdy.
Shake out the turbot —
gunmetal blue against the grey
sea and sky and gutting table.
They fall, tails flailing.
Nights on watch, tiredness
you can taste
and feel behind your eyes.
Humming refrains to unremembered songs
in the darkness,
dim light of the compass,
fingers drum the edge
of the wheelhouse window.
Water slaps the wooden hull.

Casualty
(For Don)

Early morning. St. Pierre Bank.
Gale Warning.
Waging the longest war against the oldest enemy.
Towing a cripple, fifty miles to harbour.
Ten hours, maybe twelve.
Astern, blurred in the murk:
Kenavo's navigation lights
wink, dim and lonely.

The line parts and parts again
and the radio drones melancholy tones:
Gale Warning.

A light on our quarter, the loom
of a vessel in the fog:
Emeline ghosts alongside,
takes station to starboard,
smoke blackened colours
flapping from her boom stay.
Battle Ensign.

Transported

He came alongside the stage
at Grates Cove;
three hundred pound puncheon
balanced on the tawts.

The man above rove tackles for the lift.
Impatient,
he stood and braced and bent and heaved to shift
the wooden cask up on his knees,
then straight over his head
and went on
down through the bottom of the boat.

Vexed him somethin' wicked,
before he died.

Gill Nets

Spiders
make up silken twine.
From shed eaves dangle
their webs like gill nets —
four or five in line.
And one at right angles.
Flies turn at the wall of mesh,
turn again — too near
and late —
into fatal fetter.
Spiders
strip the flesh,
mend again their gear
and wait —
yarn about the weather.

Icebergs

Icebergs don't bother with the wind.
Their deep draught
responds to current and tide.

Newfoundlanders understood.
In contrary gales
they made their schooners
fast to icebergs,
and in their cold lun,
with lowered sails,
were towed, steadily to windward.

Icebergs are not white, of course,
but veined in blue, ridged and furrowed
and lined in green and grey
like the hide of some wondrous animal,
flinging spray from its side,
snorting water from a rolling bow wave.
I've found myself
looking for eyes.

They are alive, you know.

The Moon

We were steaming hard south in December,
Northeast of Baccalieu.
Orion swaying over the bow.
Full Moon at Perigee laying down
a drung of glitter
through a black, rolling meadow of sea.
Alignment of Jupiter and Mars.
Mainmast etching long figure-eights
across the stars.
"The Moon. The Moon." he said;
the two syllable moon
of his Cape Shore accent coiling off his tongue
like a heaving line flung to windward.
"De Yankees was ashore on de Moon."
His mouth expanded sideways —
"How long would it take to steam dere,
Observer?"
"At twelve knots?
Wouldn't carry enough cigarettes, Skipper."

As Loved Our Fathers

Our graves were marked, briefly, by painted splinters.
Dying was easy work, we did it well
and often — left to our heirs: Starvation Winters
and no cost of burial or coffin.

How wrong to call us 'lost'.
We knew where we were when we drowned;
familiar names — the inshore rocks
where we were tossed,
familiar shoals on the Offer Ground.
Did we have the right to hazard our lives
to feed families we seldom saw?

Did we have the right to call
ourselves fathers, or to father them at all?

We were a succession of ghosts,
who lent our names to our children
to weight against the anonymous
ballast of mighty women who bore them
and strangely, loved us.

II

Fair Manus

The Masterless Men of the Southern Shore

Our partisans never rode horses,
raised sabres or proud battle flags.
With cutlass and long barrelled musket,
they crept o'er the barrens in rags.

For they were the men without masters,
deserters who scoffed at the law,
rebelling against King and Collar —
the worst kind of rebels of all.

For the Bible said men must have masters,
and slavery — the Will of the Lord.
And the King was God's Chosen Lieutenant
and truth was the point of a sword.

They swore they would no more be vassals,
to bastards grown rich from their trade;
escaped from the coast to the marshes,
on Butter Pot, built a stockade.

They learned from the Bush-Born and Indians,
took food from the barrens and trees.
They ate of the duck and the partridge,
the caribou, beaver and geese.

They came in the night to the outports,
and traded their furs, hides and meat,
receiving in turn what they needed;
musket balls, powder and tea.

Royal Marines sent to take them,
encumbered and lost in the fog,
grew fearful when saw there beside them,
the prints of bare feet in the bog.

For the Masterless Men were once sailors,
and sailors went barefoot, you know,
and knew what to do with the "Bloody Backs";
hated them worse than the foe.

Then one night four youngsters were taken,
who'd escaped from a ship in the bay.
In the woods, the Marines left their bedding,
and wild heather grows there today.

These young boys were hanged from the yardarm,
examples to all by their fate.
The news of it passed to the outlaws
and vengeance they knew, mustn't wait.

They came to the coast before dawning.
The frigate at anchor was moored.
And stealthily cutting her cables,
she drifted and wrecked on the shore.

The Masterless Men live forever,
our Newfoundland partisans bold,
who fought for the rights of the people.
May their memory never grow old.

April 25th

The day passes
without so much as a whimper.
A day like this in other lands
would see commemoration
or suppression of commemoration.
But in this place —
In this place, history
is carefully untaught,
memory scorned,
and even drunks are ignorant.

The eight men killed, forgotten.
They are known only to those who dig
under the manure of permitted Heritage.

Five were hanged on Belvedere Street.
Three were carried out of the country,
to Halifax — a proper garrison town
and a British colony
where they could be shot
without much noise.

And the five and the three
and the nameless others who escaped
to the Shore and the coves
and oblivion;
their ghosts still walk the coast roads
and mark their time.

They were purveyors of "infidel ideas"
we're told we never had
in the deluge of lies
about long suffering loyalty
to oppression, neglect and lunatic kings

and a past dimmed by illiteracy,
clerics and rum . . .

But for the routine drinking
in downtown St. John's bars with names
that stink of the worst of those times,
the day passes without even a whimper.

The Wages of Spring

The fever of our Springs was raised to high temperature
by the Ice in March and April, a fever for food, fuel,
work, money, adventure, the Rites of Passage,
the passage of people and ships.

Fog lifting to a world alive — Harps and Hoods,
Beaters and Bedlamers, adults and pups,
barking and bawling, the undulating ice,
like some great, rough carpet,
rising and falling, rolling and breathing, everything
breathing in the glare of white and blinding blue,
glinting Sun making jewellery
of pinnacles and pressure ridges.

Ship's hulls grinding and shuddering,
coal smoke — black and thick and greasy,
staining the sheeted sails of the Wooden Walls
above the groan of timber and hemp.
House flags and ensigns streaming
ragged and dirty and proud.
The Ironclads, nosing ahead, searching for signs.
Our Fleet. An Armada to rival Spain's.
Our Forlorn Hope, our glory, our Spring Fever.

A fever unabated by hardship, cold,
squalor, suffering, loneliness and death.
One by one, we died, alone
or in huddle knots of ten or twenty,
by the each or by the shipload,
by the Christ!
We paid for our bumper trips.
Ten thousand is a guess. We cannot know;
could not stop to write them down.

No monuments here, the memory ingrained,
part Medal of Valour,
part Death Camp tattoo.
The cost of our living.
The price of our fever.
The wages of Spring.
Or was all that
someone's dream?
Or is memory passed unspoken,
stories passed untold
from a time before
the written record of things?

Of shallops and sloops, skiffs
and schooners floundering through floes,
pushed and pulled and lifted and shifted
and hauled by crawling men,
up to their hips in the freezing sea,
clambering aboard to trim sails
or out oars in the open leads
and when the ice closed, back overboard
to dance on the dancing, dazzling whiteness,
carrying their frail vessels to the seals.
Carrying the hopes of their people ashore.

Men lost in vessels named for their wives;
    Gertrude, four dead
    Emily, five dead
    Susan, five
    Antoinette, six
    Mary, six
    Harriet, six
    Elfrida, seven
    Elizabeth, sixteen
    Margaret, twenty one

in vessels named for family;
  George, seven dead
  John and Maria, twenty four
  Brothers, twenty eight

Crushed, frozen, castaway on rotting ice —
ten women off Catalina in 1867,
twenty off Twillingate in 1869,
nothing left, but to wait for the drowning.
Blown up, scalded, fell through hatchways,
for steam in bigger ships meant new ways of dying.

It was well, we did not need to bury all these dead,
  Aurora, four
  Express, nine
  Moonlight, ten
  Speedwell, ten
  Princess, fifteen
  Village Belle, eighteen
  Hope, twenty four
  Confidence, twenty six
  Active, twenty eight
  Union, twenty eight
  Peerless, forty one

for the sea had them,
the sea and the wind and the Ice in the Spring.
And we would not have had land
enough to plant turnips
in the thin soil, only the bones of the very old
and the very young.
Small cemeteries for places settled so long.
So long, we think we've been here
forever.

And what did we do, before history caught us,
clung like lichen to the rocks?
We bartered our blood for seal oil
to light the lamps of London
while we huddled in hovels
on the seaward edge of marshes.

In 1838, our Spring Fever cost us fourteen ships
and three hundred dead. We do not know their names.
1840 was the "Spring of the *Catherine*";
1844, the "Spring of the Growlers"
1852, the "Spring of the Wadhams"
fifty ships crushed in the Ice;
1864; the "Green Bay Spring" — twenty six ships lost.

Our ice broken bones bought the wealth of Empire
for those who would not imagine our existence
while our shattered vessels planched the ocean's floor.
   Tigress, twenty one dead
   Viking, twenty four
   Deerhound, twenty eight
   Northland, thirty
   Dundannah, thirty one
   Erna, thirty six
   Emerald, thirty eight

Notches on the tally stick of Death.
We were occupied with Death
for it was our life . . . and Death
was preoccupied with us.
   Huntress, forty
   Huntsman, forty four
   Greenland, forty eight
   Lion, fifty two
   Newfoundland, seventy eight
   Southern Cross, one hundred seventy three

These few:
some for which we know the numbers.
For many, their epitaph is the simple notation;
"All Hands".
For most, there is no record.
Forever.

And what became of us in the end?
We're still here,
with the sea and the wind
and the Ice in the Spring.

Brigus Sealers' Strike, 1845

Fife and drum lead
a moving droke of gaffs
down narrow streets.

In ranks, six abreast,
three thousand men.
Canvas coats and sealskin,
wool guernseys and moleskin pants,
felt caps and fur hats,
the rhythmic tramp of boots.

March airs scrape across
the thin strings of fiddles,
sparbles and creepers ring
the frozen road as they pass.

Lashed to a longer above the sway,
Pink, White and Green
streams brazen and new.

The Copper Coloureds and the Irish —
Together,
will have their rights this day.

Free Outfits
and Berth Money reduced.

Captain Abram Kean
(1855-1945)

He was Commodore of the Sealing Fleet.
The national hero of Water Street.
My people would doff caps at meeting —
a chance for a berth in his greeting.

Was it true, he'd run his winches
from both sides —
loading seals to port
and to starboard, taking dead men
off the ice?

That it could be, is enough.
That t'was said, is enough.
What odds if it wasn't true.
A seal's pelt was worth
more than a sealer's.
Everyone knew.

Fair Manus

Night on the heaving ice.
The fleet, chain of lights
alive with the bark of men,
the grumble of winches
and somewhere along scarce seen wires
stretching into the dark;
the pained movement of pelts.

Diana lies silent.
Death and the Ice Birds are waiting her out.
Beset for twelve days,
the pack has taken her in the guts.

In the 'tween decks,
one hundred twenty five men
listen 'round seal oil lamps,
listen in the pipe smoke,
the reek and the coal dust,
listen to the sound of their vessel sinking.

There is yet time to weigh the owner's offer:
their thin and toilsome lives
for seven thousand pelts on which they sit.
Stow the seals on the ice
for the company to collect
and they will be rescued.

From around the circle of grim,
gaunt and grimy faces,
approving nods begin
to end a silent discussion.

The tacit protocol.
The old barque is a tinder box.

Fifty two years of whale oil
and seal fat have soaked her wood,
will make her a glorious pyre.
Gunpowder is stowed carelessly below.
No finer trigger can be had
and every man's thumb is on the hammer.

Who lit the torches?
Who laid the charge?
It doesn't matter.
Our people have no names.
Let merchant's History record an accident.

On Being Solicited by "Crime-Stoppers"

They called one evening.
Not for me —
just riding down the phone book.
Had I heard of them?
Who hadn't.
They were looking for supporters:
Would I get involved?
They reward those whose information
proves useful to the authorities —
Anonymously. Payment in cash.
I had heard of them.
Who hadn't.
I had thought myself safe.
Now they were in my home,
slithering in over telephone lines.
I could hear my own heartbeat.
My hand on the receiver was shaking,
but my voice was not.
Wrong time to call. Wrong person.
Reaching into the bilges
of my seagoing vernacular,
I think I made them understand
that I was not interested.
Oh, I had heard of them.
I had heard they were beaten in '45.

At the Constable Moss Memorial

Where are you now, Constable William Moss? You did more in death to set back human progress than you ever meant to, in your foreshortened life.

Just another cop in Badger, in 1959. It was cold that day. Was your blood hot? Or were you just "obeying orders", orders to beat your fellow Newfoundlanders?

Your head got in the way of a birch junk, the government said, though there are whispers that it was the flailing club of another cop, as shocked, dazed and bleeding, loggers tried to defend their picket line against a police attack.

It's too easy to say the cops were out of control, the "few rotten apples" line that serves so well. You weren't a rotten apple, Constable William Moss. Perhaps you were just put into a rotten barrel.

Struck down, however it happened, you paid the Supreme Sacrifice for the anonymous men with money, for the owners and handlers of Joe Smallwood.

You were used, Constable William Moss; mind and body, arm and hand, a hired thug, a goon, to silence with a night-stick, cries for decency.

"We are only loggers", they said. And their leader became the scapegoat for a snarling propagandist. And the cowardly politicians and their business booze buddies, the dog collars and the rest, either fell into or for, the government's line.

And you became the martyred dead. The only one. And what was proven; that loggers are tougher than cops? It isn't enough to justify your death.

But it is perhaps fitting, that softball bats now swing in a tournament named for you. Does anyone see the irony, or is that your true legacy; a stunned, brain damaged society?

You probably weren't an evil man. That's an old debate. But if this were Berlin today, or most anywhere, your crude monument would be hauled down, your hapless name reviled, your smug superiors jailed.

Gander Monument

There is a monument outside Gander
to honour the soldiers who died
when their airplane,
(Let us agree on one thing)
Fell down.
An American paratrooper
holding hands with a boy and girl.
Has he rescued them?
Or is he taking them into the woods?
If so, do not worry . . . they become,
suddenly, not our children.
Or do we still believe the Peacekeeper Lie?
U.S. troops are never Peacekeepers.
Screaming Eagles do not make good playmates.
And these, returning from the Middle East;
Whose peace did they keep?
The peace of mass graves?
The U.S. killed . . . no one knows.
Census under bombardment is haphazard.
Sixteen inch shells obliterate people.
They become suddenly . . . nonexistent.
Limbs never tally up and Body Counts
are meaningless without ears to sever.
We have erected a monument outside Gander,
to honour the soldiers who killed . . .

Canada Day

Transfer payments mean
we can afford to buy the things
our resources make
somewhere else with our power.

Occasional chastisements
from the "Globe and Mail"
mean we can even feel
grateful for the opportunity.

All this means
that explosives can be
diverted for fireworks
to celebrate all this.

Fireworks are pretty,
encourage us to look up.

So we don't see
the red maple leaves
falling from the trees.

Flags

Coloured bits of rip-stop nylon
flap from tops of shiny capped arrogant poles
before facades of government power.
Halyards locked away in tiny boxes,
lest they fall to nocturnal feats
of drunken daring, midnight lark
or daylight deeds deliberate.

Red and white of the new Master,
Red, White and Blue of the old,
and in between, the same

cold colonial rag in stark redraft
by some technocrat of the New World Order:
a hollow banner
impaled by a Golden Shaft,
pointing to our future.

Remembrance

We do not reflect
on those who gained our freedom.
We neither grieve nor respect
their legacy.
There are no wreaths for them —
just careful neglect
of their memory.

There are no parades, no tearful toasts,
nor coloured bunting flapping,
no cannonades and no Last Posts,
nor hypocrites yapping.

Free speech was never won
by dying for the bosses in trenches.
It came by fighting them at home,
exposing their pretenses.

The only freedom we have today
was won by those who fought
against those who lay
wreaths on Remembrance Day.

III

...fences on the landwash...

Come All Ye

Oh come all ye Newfoundlanders,
and harken to my song.
I trust that I will not delay ye long.
But I can no more be silent,
though voiceless I may be
to cull our future right from history's wrong.

Our resources have been bartered
in trade for promised gold,
and everything we've had now has been sold.
We've slept through a red sky morning,
awakening too late,
to try and keep the wolf outside the fold.

Well, the wolf is in the kitchen
and we're outside the door,
our Mother's rifle shattered on the floor.
And as through a smoke stained window,
we peer and wait in vain,
imagining we'll get inside once more.

We light candles in the darkness,
await the rising Sun,
and trusting in each new day when it comes.
And it's coming for us all; a new Winter of the Rals.
When everything is lost, what's to be won?

So come all ye Newfoundlanders,
we all must lend a hand,
in fighting for the future of our land.
Don't put your faith in leaders
and their platitudes and lies.
The big, black dog must growl,
the bear must rise.

Fog

Fog appears
like cavalry —
A silent, spreading spectral
host of heavy horse,
holding the high ground
for days,
or suddenly sweeping down valleys
in enveloping echelons
of ethereal grey,
curling round corners
and rolling up streets
to break
against the squares of buildings.
Here, fog occupies towns.

Fences on the Landwash

Sun drawing water;
cove like greased graphite.
Tupperware boats bounce at anchor,
stark white in the evening light.

New house suddenly built,
to gape over the coast,
larger than the landscape,
distainful of ghosts.

Five fathoms from high water
is Ours, you Motherless Oonshick!
In times ago we burned stages
that barred us from the shore.

Now we have swallowed anchors
and the wind
won't call our dances anymore.

But this is still Newfoundland,
the fog and the hungry cliffs.
And the only fences on the landwash
are bones of skiffs.

Goats

The Artist says
that no one lived there.
We must in faith, concur,
for she has looked it over
and the grade's too steep
for her to contemplate
with artless eye . . .

I recall . . . tall houses, tiers of stairs, briar roses in the gardens, cherry trees, Soldier's Pond, the rocks where Southsiders fell, trying to hold D'Iberville's army in 1696. No monuments there. He's a Canadian hero. Our people have no names.

I remember Portuguese barquentines and schooners tied up three and four abreast, their crew playing soccer on the wharves or going up the road with bread and wine. I remember rocks and hills, valleys and drokes. You needed to be a goat.

The bonfire place — rusting barrel hoops and heat-shattered rocks, evidence of Guy Fawkes fires such as we'll never see again. Ships' timbers and tar and seal oil casks, stacked twenty feet high, made into buildings. You went in a door, lit the fire inside and "lef 'er go!" Bonfires to frighten those who have always been frightened of bonfires. We didn't know we were supposed to be celebrating poor Guy's capture and not his courage.

Guns fired on New Year's Eve. And no 12 gauges, these, but long Poole Guns, heavy sealing pieces with five- and six-foot barrels that roared like rafting growlers beneath the bows of icebreakers.

You can't do that anymore. The crowd who use guns as weapons have taken power from the crowd who use guns as tools.

We had our stories . . . How they took the coal from Cashin's enormous pile — in winter when t'was froze solid. People who had slaved to unload it, now having to steal to keep warm. The Coal Bandits. All through January and February, tunnels honeycombed the mountain of coal, turning it into a hollow hill on the waterfront. Come April, when the frost went out of it — Boom! Down she came! Almost gave Old Man Cashin a heart attack.

Stealing coal from the horse wagons as they rumbled along, running behind and dodging the driver's whip . . . spreading scads of brittle ice over deep potholes, sprinkling snow to make them look solid for unwary trucks to dip their wheels and shake, with any luck, a few lumps of coal onto the road. The Southside Road.

My Father's house at the bottom of Ford's Hill. Grandfather's, high and alone, above Great-Grandfather's — where the witch lived. My Great-Grandmother. They only called her a witch out of fear and earshot. She was a Gypsy, so the polite maintained, small and dark . . . like a Beothuk.

Shawnadithit is buried on the Southside, in the old graveyard of St. Mary's, the great church with the viaduct where the river flowed underneath and we went, when brave enough, and felt with our fingers the cold, wet stones.

Stones. I remember the Stone House where the old woman sat before a fireplace, her big hooka pipe erupting in gouts of smoke like a coal-burning barque.

Or did we dream all that?

> The Artist has assured us
> that no one ever lived there
> and she for certain knows thus,
> having never been there.
> Too steep! Too steep!
> Maybe for her flattened feet.

But not for goats. That's what they called us; the goats of the Southside Hills. Bill Goats and Nanny Goats, famed forever in song:

"Oh the Billy Goat
chased the Nanny Goat
over the hill
and tore her petticoat!"

Of the seal rending plants that discouraged settlement, the Artist has not heard. Of the wind that moved vessels easier to the north side, she does not know. No grant to find out and home, after all, is where the grant is.

Of the destruction of the Southside, she cannot know, probably thinks Harbour Drive has been there forever, cannot comprehend water lapping the pilings under Bowrings and the London and every building on that side of Water Street. Cannot believe a whole community was rubbed out for rock to fill in between the wharves of Beck's Cove, Ayre's Cove, Baird's Cove and the rest. Does she wonder why these short streets are called coves? It doesn't matter.

She didn't hear the blasting nor feel
her bedroom shake from jackhammers
in the night that kept us all awake.
She didn't see clapboarded houses
stagger in the wind as foundations
were dug away to frighten those within.
She wasn't told she lived in slums,
nor threatened with the Law.
No Constable came to her door.
No Sheriff's Writ she saw.

I remember the bulldozers and the wrecking gangs and the people terrorized into selling out for a few months' rent; walls torn down when those in an adjoining house finally quit the racket and moved to the north side.

They told one that he could find a basement apartment in one of the new bungalows on Elizabeth Avenue.

"I'm not gonna live," he said, "in no one else's cellar!"

Framed on my wall hangs a yellowed paper. It's from the Exchequer Court of Canada and is the affidavit of a harried official who, under the authority of the Expropriation Act, thought he was going to "enter upon and attempt to take possession" of our house in the name of the Queen.

The Queen had to do without, that day.

"Resistance and opposition," it reads and refers to my Father, one of the "Four Just Men", Sam Chafe, Lloyd Horwood, Winnie Russell and Lindsay Benson, who stood against . . . what? Progress? Or power? Or the progress of power? Stubborn, but they were goats.

On the other side, the usual array of well-dressed scab herders and legislative shakedown artists, courts, cops and clergy, Rex Renouf and Billy Browne. Renouf? Our MHA. Well, someone's MHA.

"Enough of O Nuff!" said the goats.

The Honourable William J. Browne. Solicitor General for Canada, MP Against St. John's West, admirer of Mussolini and Franco. His name might have been Billy, but he was no goat.

We were the last family below the Long Bridge.

There is a certain retroactive pride in loneliness but all we felt that last winter was cold. Our house was reduced to a reeling crate with three sides and the March wind ripped through the blankets, cardboard and tarpaulins put up to block it. We were alone.

But we got money for our home, real money, enough to start again and we walked out that Spring morning, past the wrecked and abandoned houses, through the snow and the mud and the shattered world we hardly recognized and the Big Shots and the arse lickers knew who we were.

The houses had to be left, property of the Canadian government, the materials to be sold on the legalized Black Market by connected contractors.

But stories . . . People coming back in the night, gutting their homes, stealing back what was stolen from them; taking the fixtures, wood, tiles, even shagged off with the toilet, left curtains in the windows so, looking up from the road, no one could tell . . .

I return to the Southside Hills sometimes . . . in March when skeins of ice glint on the horizon, ribbons of ivory 'twixt wind and water, passing slowly as time once did. I try to remember . . . houses . . . people's faces . . . .

> Old gardens, soft white patches
> on black rock, glisten
> in the bright, cold Sun of Spring.
> Alders alter the land,
> hide scars and stone fences —
> a chequerboard where no one plays.
> Abandoned wells — frozen moons
> shine translucent
> from ruins above the road.
> Icicles drape down cliffs —
> Conkerbells, thick
> and solid as longshoremen.
> Stunted cherry trees
> of forgone cultivation
> bend away from the wind . . .

I suppose we bent too. But we didn't break. Stubborn as goats. I still paw the ground.

But I don't keep my head down.

On Water Street, a tourist asks directions . . . to the Southside.

"Well," I answer, for this is my time, "turn left at the Long Bridge."

It's long gone, but I mention it anyway, for his education and my peace of mind.

"No. Go South on Water Street. Toward the West End. The West End is in the South. The East End is in the North. It's got to do with magnetic compasses . . .

51

"There. Turn left on that railway overpass. No. The railway's gone. You see the sign? Cape Spear. National Historic Park. No. There's nothing there. It means nothing. The most easterly point in the New World? If you don't count half of Brazil. The most easterly point in North America? If you don't count Greenland. Just old gun batteries, a lighthouse and fog. A good place to slip off the rocks. What do you want to see the ocean for anyway? Due east is Ireland? Never see a map of the world? Due east from Cape Spear is France, b'y.

"Don't drive up the hill, turn left on the Southside Road and head back along the harbour. Fine houses? That's all there's left. Used to be houses right to Fort Amherst. Everything below the Long Bridge is gone and so is that. See that mound. Used to be a massive stone church. They say the last of the Beothuks is buried there. They say she was the last of the Beothuks. And that's as much as they knows about it.

"Up over the hill, there's ponds where people used to swim. There's places where you can't see Cabot Tower, the city or the sea; you'd think you were on the barrens somewhere. It's higher than Signal Hill.

"You know were Whitten's Store used to be? Where the Downtons lived. The Lythgoes. The Ebsarys? My Father worked here, loading salt and coal, breaking his back when he should have been in school.

"Our house? It was at the bottom of Ford's Hill. We had two front gardens, terraced, with steps running up the middle. You wouldn't know a house was ever there, if you wouldn't know. It's all gone now, the hill is like someone took an axe to it. Most of our land is at the bottom of the harbour, on the north side, under Harbour Drive, maybe under the heritage railway car. No. There was never a railway on the waterfront. It's just a tacky tourist trinket, the type of thing politicians are apt to do when they're desperate to justify a hangover.

"Bitter? My son, I was vinegar before I was five.

"Keep going. There. That dry ditch was Bowrings River. The old sealers used to tie up here. The Wooden Walls. Ever hear about them? Three-masted barques with auxiliary steam engines, burning good Welsh anthracite when they could get it; Yankee Slack when they couldn't; the Skipper's furniture when they had to. The Wooden Walls of Newfoundland. They're long gone. The last one was *Eagle.* Belonged to Bowrings. The owners towed her out and burned her in 1950, scuttled her in a hundred fathoms in the Cordellia Deeps off Cuckhold's Head — a fitting name. Harry Burton, from Greenspond, wrote a poem about her:

"Here Atlantic's foam wreaths float
In aqua-floral tribute to a ship submerged . . ."

"There's the Imperial Oil Wharf. In 1942, a big fire, a black pall covered everything. Flames blasted out through the greasy smoke that shrouded the whole hill, fuel drums flying everywhere.

"A tug — the Skipper took her in until her bows touched the pilings. They lashed her there with wire and fought the fire, tied to the burning wharf. *Tenacity.* That was her name. Ever hear about that?"

The old Southsiders graze where they can now. Most of them are dead. And with each year passing, their mark on this place fades further from view and from memory. Time will erase their legacy. Time and the alders.

But we lived there once. Already, there are those who say that no one ever did.

They? Who are they? Them that don't know; them that always got their faces goin'.

But I don't know much.

I was told, one night in a downtown bar. Someone had said I didn't sound like a Newfoundlander, didn't say the sort of things that Newfoundlanders say. What was my name? Where was I from?

"Benson,", I said. "St. John's," I said. "The Southside originally."

"Ye're not from de Sout'side!"

An old man I hadn't noticed before, sitting at a table behind me, thrust his great jibboom of a nose into the conversation.

"Ye're not from de Sout'side!" He roared his triumphant truth and I was caught in the most damnable lie a Newfoundlander can tell.

"Sure ye're only t'ird generation. Johnny-Come-Lately! Yeer Great Gran'fadder came in from Grates Cove. Yeer Gran'mudder was a Carter from Greenspond. Yeer Mudder came in from Grand Bank. Sout'side? G'way ye Bayman!"

It was true. What could I know about the place, except stories?

And I was only five when we left.

I'm living up the Southern Shore now, in Tors Cove. I take my daughter to the landwash, in the woods, up to a hill that was her favourite place. She is five, but is already learning the price of the progress of power.

They have gouged out her memory, dug from it a hill she called "Butterfly World"; briar roses, partridgeberries, strawberries, green; paradise impaled on a front-end loader, her "secret" playground disfigured for a gravel pit — landfill for somewhere else.

She is saddened by what has happened and asks me why. We sit, eating berries. I rub the juice across our cheeks to honour the Little Men and tell her the stories of goats.

She says she will remember . . . and never let anyone say that no one ever played here.

> "Oh the Nanny Goat
> chased the Billy Goat
> over the hill
> and tore her petticoat!"

Beach Glass

Wandering the strand, I search
beneath the ballycatters
for toughened, coloured beach glass
in the sand.
Among the waving beach grass,
spiders scurry over stones
and the wind moans legends;
of Englishmen's laws to drive us from the coast
with whips and iron brands to teach
the livyeres to keep back six miles or more,
so as not to interfere with those each Summer,
who came to fish from stages on the shore.

Gazing out the bay, eyes sweep
beyond the ballycatters
to the island's yellowed beach grass.
Grey waves pound the beach glass.
Shards return like forbears' bones
and the wind moans prophecies:
Canadian laws to drive us from the coast
with gates and iron bars to teach
the livyeres to keep back as in old tales,
so as not to interfere with those each Summer,
who frame the cliffs, the icebergs and the whales.

Backbone

We saw it on the landwash,
a vertebrae in seaweed shroud.

To my eye, soft and warm,
almost alive, it seemed
light enough to lift,
bring home,
finish what polishing
tides had done.

But it was hard and cold
and gleamed
and more than my puny strength
could shift.

And looking close;
saw pistons, valves and shaft
half buried there.
Could almost tell
it was an In-Line Six,
ripped from some lost craft
and carried here
by the unrelenting swell.

Colours

Mediterranean colours
wrung from pastel grapes,
and bottled on the Cote d'Azur,
washed on the rolling granite
of this place
in shades the barrens never knew,
the landwash never sees;
impotent impressions
by artless artistries.

No smell of fog or taste of bog,
no ear for the rote,
no eye for shore or tuckamore,
no words to the songs,
nor music in the notes.

Incredibly, indelibly,
infallibly to show,
the isolated artists
and the land they do not know.

Caplin Weather

They passed through our gear,
three hundred miles east of Cape Spear.
In June, when the days
were mauzy and sad.
Mauzy in calm, or in forty knots,
You fear you'd go crazy,
if you weren't already mad.

On the beach, in the sand,
dress tied up to her thighs,
long, strong wet legs
greeting each shift of tide,
my wife has them in dipnets,
long before we land.

Each shining fish, her pride,
and the sea's fleeting gift
for our lost Summer —
thin silver in her hand.

Gun Control

In rooms of my parents' house,
rifles stood in corners
with brooms.
Shotguns leaned behind the kitchen door,
cartons of rounds
in the pantry drawer, empty casings
of .22s, kept for target practice.

In the woods, we talked
with the wind and birds and dogs,
built boughwhiffens,
walked the narrow forest pathways,
found under logs, berries
only children
and "Little Men" could eat,
Sallies, snapdragons,
clover sucked between our teeth.

Following the dogs we strayed
'cross barrens.
I was never led to be afraid
of Distemper or trees
shaken by the wind or harsh
evenings, low and moonless on the marsh.

I remember my first gun, when I was twelve.
I keep it in a rack secured
until my children speak of it and ask
if they can learn to use it —
another tool, with the axe and hammer;
safe but within view.

I will not keep from sight, anything
to tempt young desires for the hidden,
the strange or forbidden.

I will not countenance a fright
manufactured by liars.

Gun control is no game of skill
for wet politicians, manipulating
the thought control market.
Gun control is hitting your target.

And eating what you kill.

Though such might call us
savages for what we eat
as they sup with mankind's butchers
on stolen meat.

In rooms of my parents' house,
rifles stood in corners with brooms.

Beach Spider

Scravelling for stones for garden drains.
Before my outstretched hands,
a tall boot fains to block the Sun.
Raising my head to curious eyes —
a spider exposed — I nod and scutter away.
Who is brave on their knees?

I see her confident boots
yield to the slippery rocks,
camera's careful sway,
hair flattened by the breeze.

Away down the beach,
companions gawk at icebergs.
No yarns for them this day;
brief shame, a baulk at my words.

Again alone, I watch them
stare out to sea,
enjoy their money spent,
before the evening is through.
I clutch my yaffle of stones
and wonder how long it will be
before police are sent to stop me
stealing their view.

Berry Picking Time to Come

Young women with old eyes
wave to wayward youngsters,
warn in windborne whispers:
"Don't stray now!"
Old woman in young guise,
fingers like crunnicks, hair askew,
backs bent in the duckishness,
scravel for illicit blue.

Flattened to lichen on higher ground,
young men cradle old rifles,
deafened by the sound
of their own heartbeats,
counting the cost of the call,
as the wind drives away the smell of fear.

The people, like the barrens —
stark and near;
grown hard in the frost of the Fall.

IV

Winter of the Rals

Nanny

My Grandmother belonged to Greenspond;
a half-tide, treeless, rock-strewn
hump of waterlogged marsh in Bonavista Bay.
A small, dark, wire-wound woman
with a spine of juniper,
and a family tree of tuckamore.

I asked her once where her people came from,
and back through years, we copied on islands:
Ship Island, Newell's, Puffin, Pool's,
and still, nowhere from Greenspond.
Her people were from the islands.
They hunted seals.

"But where were they from, Across?"
"Across?"
"You know. Across. England."

She rounded on me, brown eyes burning
in contempt or bewilderment or both.
Buried beneath the memory
of those who fought West Countrymen
for control of the shore,
lay some sudden and submerged Beothuk
progenitor who did not understand.
"Never came from there. Englishmen over there!"

Her people were from the islands.
They hunted seals.

The Patriot

"This night we proclaim ourselves a
people! We proclaim our nationality!"

Robert John Parsons
June 15, 1840

Do not seek this Patriot's bones
in some weedy cemetery,
where the wind obliterates stones.
Nor seek his face in some place of revelry,
in copper gone verdigris.

Do not seek him among the green,
his spirit there, no crumbling tomb encase,
but where the stark wind stalks unseen,
defining and divining This Place.

No monuments here stand,
in memory of our own,
no iron to steel the nerve,
when we, our fate recind.
What, in another land,
might well have been his stone,
will one day better serve
as ballast against the wind.

Winter of the Rals

Eighteen Sixteen. The year after the wars ended. "The Year With No Summer". A volcano, erupting from around the world, darkened the skies of north Europe and people shivered and the rich wondered if their God had abandoned them and the poor wondered what t'was all about.

In Newfoundland, the fishery collapsed. And when the Ice came in the Spring, it stayed. From every headland, the world beyond was white and for those who moved under canvas, for whom every country was just beyond the horizon, there was sudden isolation.

It was cold. Food was short for nothing could be brought in and nothing would grow under the frozen wind. St. John's, on the edge of famine, blocked with outport refugees from American raids, St. John's burned. Houses, stores, stages, flakes, wharves, vessels. Everything.

Fire and Ice in awful combination.

The time for Summer came. No one noticed. It was cold and the jury-rigged town burned again in the Fall. Come Winter, t'was said to be a poor lookout.

Starving people, bleary ey'd in rags, in blankets, in the streets, scravelled to find anything to eat, fought to eat what they found.

Rals, they were called. Rowdies. History says that the people were fearful. But the Rals were the fearful people.

Shifting Demographics

Here, old men in greatcoats
and buttondown hats
lean on benches and yarn.
Little left to do at this stage.

Who remembers the Coves?
Clift-Baird's, Becks and Ayre's,
when they were coves and the harbour
waters passed beneath Long Bridge.

Who remembers the fish mongers?
Their wooden barrows?
Thrusting cod, big as dogs
under the high noses of passers-by
on Water Street,
when the smell of fish in the Sun
was not alien to the young.

Who remembers *Ungava* and *Imogene*?
(One and two for the heaviest load)
Thetis and *Algerine*?
(Bloody flippers carried up the road)

Who remembers when the Longshoremen
ruled the waterfront
and the LSPU was strong?
("Like peas set in concrete")
Wages were high, unemployment was low,
because Solidarity was a creed.

Here, the old men sit, thankful
to have been born
in a time that allows them to die
without a struggle.

For here, it's minimum wage,
firing on the spot,
no unions and no recourse.
And here there is no industry;
even the building is owned Upalong.

No one makes anything here
(besides not enough money)
and no one notices
fluorescent lights
have scrambled their brains.

The busses swing in, disgorge the hurried
buyers, the lookers and touchers,
swallow the harried plastic bag clutchers
and swing away to the drizzly suburbs.

But here, it never rains.
Getting wet,
means sitting too near the fountain.
Being wet,
means something else.

Here, the old men gather like crows
near the entrance — no benches outside.
And they cannot smoke their pipes
in the Mall.

Veteran

He'd heard it said:
"There are no atheists in foxholes."
by people who did not
count with the dead,
who tried to fix some meaning
to the bloody farce,
who wouldn't know a foxhole
from a dog's arse.

Irving Fogwill
(1901-1984)

I found my way to you without a chart,
feeling ahead with leadline,
watching the birds and clouds,
the colour of water,
shouting echoes from cliffs
within a shroud of fog.

That your name was unmentioned in schools,
I should have expected,
from soulless sycophants and fools,
for you were Newfoundland's greatest poet,
and therefore never could disturb
the dreams of unrequited colonials.

Instead, I learned that poetry
consisted of beating bleating nouns
about the head with blunt adjectives;
that esoteric was generic
and interpretation: education.

That we could produce poets in this place,
wasn't a notion.
Unthinkable, perhaps,
that an ocean could inspire.

So I found you on my own —
and ran hard aground on your words.

A Brighter Tomorrow

Along the black patched and potholed pavement
the bungalows squat like jaded
Line Dancers in faded makeup.
A strip; the hopeful and the important call a town.
Wrecks of fridges and cars,
like rotted teeth of children on the ridges
of gravel pits and fringes of oily waste ground,
offering wan smiles and downcast eyes
to motor driven tourists.

Mothers bawl: "Come home to yer Supper!"
Have seen twice their years go by each day.
Thirty-For-Sixty tonight and maybe
twenty bucks from a neighbour's husband later on . . .
will buy milk tomorrow.

Outside the store, young men's t-shirted arms
fold in sullen self embrace.
"Got a job. On the Mainland. Goin' next week."
"Tha's all ya can do."
"Back Christmas, maybe."

I Call Her My Penelope

For she is fleet and sure and beautiful
and strong,
(but tougher than she is strong)

Her speech to friends:
eloquent, urgent, compassionate.
Her speech to foes:
point blank and well directed.

She knows what she is about
and does not shrink from odds.

Like Ulysses' wife, she lives near the sea,
weaves and is faithful,
awaits a sailor gone too long.

I call her my Penelope,
after a ship.

A Long Run Home

A hundred miles or a thousand,
it's always a long run home.
A time to sleep, to dream
vividly to pass the time.

Watches and tea, maybe a song,
following stars to a Long Run home.

Land rises black
from a black horizon,
becomes known shapes;
cliffs and capes
and lights where people live,
lights where my love waits.
Or is she sleeping
and dreaming vividly?

A long run to Long Run,
a warm home in a cold cove
and a bed
wide enough for two.

The Island

The island is fading by half measures
and lame, the snivellous inmates hobble about,
mumble their leader's claim
that things will be different;
once they've done more of the same.

Their politics, an ethereal circus,
they give their allegiance to clowns,
rant at the injustice of myths
and thought is out of bounds.

Deaf to all but the call to vote for their enemies,
deaf even to the rote, unheard in the din
on monotonous mundanity,
prey to the whim of political inanity,
false assumption from prepared presumption,
they are strapped in the coats
of popular misconsumption,
blind and no longer see the wind.

Afterword

And We Were Sailors

And pirates and smugglers and outlaws
and rebels and mummers and wreckers
and salvers and shepherds and witches
and healers and hunters of birds and bears,
caribou and seals and fish and great whales
and there is magic in us.

The magic of fog and wind and sea and ice,
boggy ponds and peat lined gullies,
barrens and marshes and gnarled woods,
shapes and colours changing in the dusk
and dawn — blue hills and purple bracken
and shadows — of stunted, wind blasted trees;
crunnick and starrigan and tuckamore.
Shadows of people:
our men were able and strong
but our women were mighty.

We know the sky, the tides and the moon's power.
Our houses feel the fingers of the wind
and stairs creak with the tread of dripping fetches —
our people lost at sea.

From off black headlands, their schooners
stand on now, against the gales,
are manned by crews whose bones are food for fish.
Ghosts walk here
and here gallop the dogs of lore.
We listen in the darkness.
The rote from the barrisway — the sea's rote,
constant . . . like background music,
a tune familiar, that will not die.

Listen . . .
Listen . . .
Mark what ye have heard.

Glossary of Words

Ballycatter	Ice formed by spray and wave action, fast to the shore.
Barque	Three masted vessel, square rigged on fore and mainmasts, fore and aft rigged on mizzenmast.
Barrisway	Sand bar across the bottom of a cove, forming a saltwater pond behind it.
Beach Glass	Shards of broken pottery and glass, worn smooth by wave action.
Beater	A three week old Harp seal, capable of swimming.
Bedlamer	Year old Harp seal.
Beothuk	Aboriginal inhabitants of Newfoundland.
Berth Money	Money paid to ship owner by sealer who wished to work in the vessel.
Boughwhiffen	Igloo shaped house, built of boughs.
Brin	Burlap.
Conkerbells	Icicles.
Copied	Jumped from ice pan to ice pan, before the pan sank under one's weight.

Copper Coloured	A 19th century Anglo-Irish term of contempt for Newfoundlanders, due to their swarthy features, an allusion to their (at that time well known) Beothuk ancestry. Also called "Bush Born" from their being born in their "Winterhouses" in the forest.
Creepers	Iron gang spikes, fitted to the soles of boots for purchase on ice.
Crime Stoppers	Organization encouraging anonymous paid informers.
Crosshanded	Alone.
Crunnick	A Starrigan, cut or broken up for firewood. Branches of a Starrigan.
Cutlass	Seaman's sword.
Droke	Grove of trees, especially in narrow valley.
Drung	Narrow laneway.
Duckish	Twilight, usually in the evening but also in the morning.
Fetch	Ghost of a person which appears to family and friends when that person is dying.
Finisterre	Most westerly cape of northern Spain.

Flake	Wooden platform on which fish is spread to dry.
Flipper	Shoulder of seal, prized by Newfoundlanders and Inuit as delicacy.
Gannetize	To eat voraciously. From Gannets, large and seemingly greedy sea birds, which will actually take food out of the mouths of other birds.
Glitter	Coating of ice on trees, fences, etc.
Globe and Mail	Right wing, city newspaper in Toronto, Ontario.
Growler	Low lying iceberg, particularly dangerous to vessels.
Gullies	Series of small, linked ponds.
Guernsey	Woolen sweater.
Harp	Type of hair seal hunted in Newfoundland, Labrador, Greenland, Norway, etc., so called from the harp shaped patch on the back of adult animals.
Hood	Type of hair seal hunted in similar areas to the Harp, so called from the skin bladder or "hood" on the head of the male.
Ironclad	Steel steam sealing ship, to differentiate from the older, wooden, auxiliary steam

	sailing vessels known as the Wooden Walls.
Juniper	Deciduous tree, elsewhere called Larch or Tamarack.
Junk	Short piece of wood.
Landwash	Seashore, usually that part of the shore between high and low tide.
Little Men	Fairies, wood elves, etc.
Livyere	Permanent inhabitant. From "live ye here". Same as "Habitant" in Quebec.
Longer	Long, narrow, tapering pole used to build flakes and stages.
Long Run	Road leading from a community, such as Long Run in Tors Cove.
LSPU	Longshoremen's Protective Union.
Lun	Shelter. On the leeward side.
Mainland	A term used by colonialist Newfoundlanders to describe Canada.
Manus	Mutiny. Forcing a Captain to give up a voyage. Strike at sea by seamen, especially sealers.
Mauzy	Rainy, drizzly and foggy weather.
Moleskin	Shaved cotton.

Mummer	Disguised participant in Christmas festivities, often used in the 19th century as a cover for political attacks.
Offer Ground	The ground further off the shore.
Penelope	Wife of Ulysses in Homer's epic poem. Also a Napoleonic Era, 36 gun frigate commanded by Henry Blackwood and a World War II light cruiser.
Planch	To floor over. Floorboards.
Oonshick	The "Chief" Mummer. According to tradition, the Oonshick is rude, pompous and arrogant, yet cannot be criticized for fear of punishment.
Pink, White and Green	Vertical tricolour formed in March, 1843, combining the pink (copper colour - faded red ochre) of the Newfoundland "Bush Born" and the green of the immigrant Irish with white to symbolize peace between, to unite all as Newfoundlanders.
Port	Left side of a vessel.
Ral	Rowdy person, vagabond.
Rote	Noise associated with the movement of the sea on the shore.
Sallies	Sheep Sorrel (Rumex Acetoscella). The leaf is chewed by children.

Schooner	Two masted vessel, fore and aft rigged on both fore and mainmasts.
Scravel	To move while in a squat or crouched position.
Screaming Eagles	Nickname of 101st Airborne Infantry Division, U.S. Army.
Shallop	Partly decked sailing and rowing boat of about 30-40 feet (10-12 metres) fitted with two masts and rigged with lugsails.
Skiff	Undecked (open) boat of 20-40 feet (7-12 metres) pulling six oars or rigged with sails, schooner fashion.
Sloop	One masted vessel, rigged fore and aft.
Smallwood	J.R. Smallwood, Premier of Newfoundland, appointed by the Canadians in 1949, continually elected and ruling with little opposition until 1972.
Sparble	Sparrow bill. Iron spike fitted to boot sole to gain greater purchase on ice.
Stage	Wooden structure for tying up boats and as a platform for fishing premises.
Starboard	Right side of a vessel.
Starrigan	Wind stripped tree.

Tarpulin	Waterproof canvas.
Tawts	Thwarts. Cross benches in a rowing boat.
Thirty-For-Sixty	"All or Nothing" bid in the popular card game of One Hundred and Twenties.
Toronto	City on large pond called Lake Ontario in the historically isolated centre of Canada.
Tuckamore	Stunted spruce or juniper, growing horizontally and thickly interwoven to form a virtual carpet on the barrens.
Ulysses	Roman name of Odysseus, wandering sailor of Homer's epic poem.
Upalong	North America.
Water Street	Financial district of St. John's.
Weltschmerz	(German) Pain of the world.
West Countrymen	Men from the Western counties in England, migratory fishermen who came to Newfoundland each Summer, returning in the Fall.
Yaffle	Armful.

Publication Credits

And We Were Sailors was recorded on the cd "We Will Remain" and broadcast on CBC Radio.

The Wages of Spring was read at the Newfoundland Historical Society's Symposium on the Seal Fishery in May, 1998 and a shorter version was published in *The Downhomer*.

The Masterless Men of the Southern Shore won First Place in the *TickleAce* Traditional Ballad Competition in 1997 and was published in *TickleAce 33* and *The Southern Post*.

The Patriot and Transported were published in *The Compass*.

Is My Love Cold? was published in *The Newfoundland Herald*.

Backbone was published in *The Gaspereau Review* (Nova Scotia).

Beach Glass was published in *The Downhomer* and *The Newfoundland Herald*.

Fair Manus was published in *The Downhomer*.

Come All Ye was recorded on the cd "We Will Remain".

Canada Day was published in an earlier version in *Semiotext* (New York).

Colours was published in *Arts Atlantic* (PEI).

Captain Abram Kean, Gill Nets and Goats were published in *TickleAce 38*.

Beach Spider was published in *The Peace Accord Newsletter* and broadcast on CBC Radio.

A Brighter Tomorrow, Flags, April 25th, and Remembrance were published in earlier versions in *Beg, Borrow or Steal*.

At The Constable Moss Memorial was a winner in the Milton Acorn People's Poetry Competition in 1996 and published in *People's Poetry Letter*.

Beach Woman and Brigus Sealers' Strike were published in earlier versions in *Ore* (England).

On Being Solicited by Crime Stoppers was published in *Seen*.

Isolation, Tail of the Bank and Iced Up were published in *The Coaster*.

Shifting Demographics was a winner in the 2000 People's Political Poetry Competition, published in *People's Poetry Letter* and broadcast on CBC Radio.

Irving Fogwell was published in *The Telegram*.

The Island was turned down for publication in *The Telegram* as it is "political" but was published in *The Newfoundland Herald*.